gaetano
pesce

gaetano
pesce

COMPACT **DESIGN** PORTFOLIO

BY MARISA BARTOLUCCI

EDITED BY MARISA BARTOLUCCI + RAUL CABRA

CHRONICLE BOOKS
SAN FRANCISCO

Design by Raul Cabra and Betty Ho
for Cabra Diseño, San Francisco.

Library of Congress Cataloging-
in-Publication Data available.

ISBN 0-8118-3788-2

Manufactured in China.

Distributed in Canada
by Raincoast Books
9050 Shaughnessy Street
Vancouver, British Columbia V6P 6E5

10 9 8 7 6 5 4 3 2 1

Chronicle Books LLC
85 Second Street
San Francisco, California 94105
www.chroniclebooks.com

FRONT COVER: UP SERIES LA MAMMA ARMCHAIR
WITH BALL OTTOMAN, 1969

BACK COVER: WAN-CHAI CHAIR, 1986–87

PAGES 1 AND 3: PRATT CHAIR SERIES, 1984

PAGE 2: PRATT CHAIR DRAWING, 1983

PAGE 4: GREEN STREET CHAIR, 1984

PAGE 6: GAETANO PESCE, 1991

Acknowledgments

Were it not for the cheerful diplomacy of Kristina Rastrom, this book may not have happened. Thank you Kristina for helping to make it so. I am grateful as well to Michael Sorkin, Murray Moss, Wendy Joseph, George Beylerian and Doug Fitch for giving me their time and thoughts about the maestro. I am indebted to Alan Rapp at Chronicle Books for his steadfast support under trying circumstances. Appreciation goes once more to Betty Ho for her inspired design work. My gratitude to Raul Cabra, my editorial partner in this series, for the intelligence, imagination, and amiability he brings to projects. Finally, thank you Judge Joe Brown for always being an option.

Gaetano Pesce: **Transgressive Design**

By Marisa Bartolucci

If Gaetano Pesce were to impart the story of his life and work, it would not be through the glossy pages of a little book like this. Such a medium would be too fixed, too finite, too uniform, too monotonous, too planned, and too damned rigid. A maestro of alchemical reactions, Pesce might instead present you with a small glass flask crudely cast in the shape of his head. When the top was pulled off, out would escape some magical vapor, redolent perhaps of minestrone, earthy, inviting, rich in ingredients. A single whiff would send you off on a vertiginous whirl of autobiographical sights, smells, and sounds: a child on a mother's lap, a Beethoven piano sonata, the Seagram Building, a fragrant gardenia, the screech of a machine, gondolas rocking in a canal, the Golgotha chair, resinous fumes, the foot of Michelangelo's *David,* a great doorway in the shape of a naked ass in a shitting crouch, a gunshot, Duchamp's *Fountain,* the stink of putrid meat, samba music, the taste of lemon ice, the gardens of the Tuilleries, the creak of a prison door, a crumpled, jelly-soft, red chair . . .

As unexpectedly as these hallucinatory vapors appeared, they would condense into a liquid, red and mercurial, pool on the ground, and then spontaneously congeal and expand into a rubbery armchair, its back the face of Pesce himself. After this mad rush of delicious and disturbing sensations and wild transmutations, you would likely collapse into the chair from exhaustion—and collapse you would, because it would have no seat. The chair would then dissolve into thin air. With a thump, you would have experienced one of Pesce's "little shocks." All you would possess from this giddy ride would be the memory of it, and as memories are subjective, this encounter with Pesce's life would in the end be shaped by you. Ecce Gaetano Pesce.

Labels like "designer," "architect," "artist" slip off this man. If it didn't sound so pretentious, "creator" might better serve, since with each project Pesce spins off fresh worlds. As Murray Moss, proprietor of the premier New York design store Moss, puts it: "With Pesce there are no insignificant projects. Every one is complete; every one as revealing of his thinking as a retrospective." **What is extraordinary about this man is not just the totality of his creations, but their determined originality and diversity. In an introduction to the catalogue of his first art exhibition in 1956, when a mere seventeen, he brashly declared "the right to be incoherent." He still lives and labors by this youthful credo, believing that today "to be" means to live in "infinite, and often contradictory ways."**[1] This stance, while often infuriating, and sometimes self-destructive, has endowed him with a protean freedom, permitting him to rove early in his career into theatrical stagings, film making, and musical composition, and later—deeply, brilliantly—into the often playful study of contemporary materials and production methods. It has enabled him to embrace the dialectical, to propose new notions of beauty, to challenge the conventional at every turn, and to attack all manner of projects from the serving dish to the city plan.

But such singularity has had its costs. With work that defies easy categorization, he has been a difficult subject for the American press to understand. Credit for charting and colonizing new realms has often gone to others. So while he is revered for his genius among an international elite of designers, artists, collectors, and critics, Pesce doesn't share the same celebrity as, say, a Frank Gehry, or the same name recognition as Ettore

Sottsass. Nevertheless, the design cognoscenti compare him to both, especially Gehry, another artist/architect who has pushed materials to their expressive limit.

A true citizen of the world, Gaetano Pesce keeps homes in New York, Venice, Paris, and Salvador, Brazil, but he remains in his essence Italian. He was born in 1939 in the northern port city of La Spezia, where his father, Vittorio, a naval officer, was stationed. Shortly after Pesce's birth, his father was killed in the war. His mother, Alda, a concert pianist, was forced to raise and support Gaetano and his two older siblings, a brother and a sister, alone, with the help of her extended family. Pesce spent his childhood shuttling back and forth between his mother's kin in the ancient cities of Este and Padua and his father's in Florence.

Wherever he was, he was in the company of women, his mother, her cousin, his paternal grandmother. Pesce admired women, especially his mother. "In Italy at that time," he says, recalling his childhood, "being a woman and the sole breadwinner for a family was not at all easy." Apparently being his mother was not easy, either. He was an adversarial child and was constantly being expelled from schools. In desperation, his mother enrolled him briefly in a convent academy for girls. There he was happy, and soon charmed the mother superior. She was among the first of many conquests. (Women have always found Pesce, with his deep empathy for the feminine and his air of dark, moody mystery, *affascinato*.)

Recalling his hardscrabble childhood, Pesce says it was "conversations about music and art that helped us survive." These conversations also helped him develop his own early artistic convictions. He remembers his mother explaining that composers like Bach, Vivaldi, and Mozart were the popular entertainers of their day; they shouldn't, she told him, be placed on a pedestal of high art. Later he would discover the same was true of the Renaissance masters. "Did you know," says Pesce, "that Leonardo was the party planner for Francis I? Look at the work of Raphael and the clothing he painted. He was a great fashion designer!" This realization that great artists could express themselves in ways that were alternatively lofty, utilitarian, and even frivolous deeply impressed him.

During his teenage years, Pesce became fascinated by Pittura Metafisica and Surrealism, especially the works of Duchamp and Dali; many of their concerns and motifs would later emerge transformed in his own work. **Nevertheless, at seventeen, reacting against the expressive improvisation of Art Informel, he and some friends banded together to make art grounded in the mathematical and scientific. Calling themselves Gruppo N, they were the first in Italy, and one of a number of recently formed "groups" in Europe, devoted to the kind of collaborative "programmed research" once practiced at the Bauhaus.** No sooner had they formed, than they began receiving gallery shows.

Most young artists who attain this kind of early recognition forswear further schooling and embark on full-time careers. But Pesce wanted to go to architecture school, he says, because "architecture was the most complex of all the arts." He traces his interest back to his early exposure to music, which, he says, "is all about space." In 1959, he enrolled at the University of Venice's Faculty of Architecture. But like many of his contemporaries, he found the rationalist architecture being taught there reductionist and oppressive. The "Modulor Man" of Le Corbusier was a sibling of socialism's "Mass Man," and Pesce considered both attempts to standardize humanity in form and inclination equally repellent.

Profoundly suspicious of socialism, Pesce decided to see it for himself and, in 1959, went off with a couple of friends on a road trip to Moscow. He vividly remembers the miserable conditions ("People were living like animals"), but what shocked him and his comrades most was what they discovered en route. While driving through Germany, they took a side trip to Dessau to visit the first site of the Bauhaus and discovered it had been converted by the East Germans into a coal room. "You could still see the terra-cotta walls of Klee's classroom," says Pesce,"but it was filled with black."

In 1961 Pesce quit Gruppo N. "Being in the group," he explains, "didn't allow me to express myself, especially to participate in the political realities of the day." This didn't stop all his collaborations, however. It gave him more time in fact for his creative sparring with Milena Vettore, a student at the experimental Venice College of Industrial Design, where Mario Bellini, Carlo Scarpa, and Richard Sapper were teaching. Pesce audited classes there. While still in school, the two set up a small studio in Padua to work on design projects. "Milena's mind was much more related to functional design," recalls Pesce. "Design alone was not enough for me. I thought objects should be about more than function." They should have meaning.

Pesce also believed architecture should be expressive of its times, not ossified in the future of the past as he felt Modernist architecture now was. He had begun thinking about a new kind of architecture that was not rational, mechanical, abstract, in other words, masculine in its values, but was pliant, mysterious, carnal, feminine. He was now convinced that real creation came out of the innovation of techniques and materials. **But in architecture school, he was only being taught about traditional approaches. So on his own he went to visit chemical factories to learn about the day's most exciting materials—plastics. In all their diversity, their malleability, their sensitivity, their alchemical mystery, plastics offered the young designer myriad new forms of expression. In them, Pesce found his medium, his metier, his mission.**

In 1964 Pesce met Cesare Cassina of the eponymous contemporary furniture company, one of the industry's leaders. Impressed by Pesce's precocious vision, Cassina offered him a monthly stipend to continue his research and travel. He also invited him, if he wanted, to work on new products for the company. It was an extraordinary gift, as was the friendship that developed. "Cassina became a kind of father to me," says Pesce. "He was a simple, very practical man, but he had a very sophisticated mind. Through him I learned a lot about factory production." After graduating in 1965 Pesce traveled around Europe and spent time in Finland, then a hot spot for contemporary design. He then moved his studio to Paris.

"I left Italy because I had to discover something else," he says. "From the point of view of everyday life, it was in the grip of politics. You had to have party papers to work at certain places. I felt more free, more alive, abroad." But he felt directionless creatively. "I wasn't doing much. I did some prints," he remembers. "Art didn't give me much energy."[2] Perhaps, because he wasn't sure how to make it anymore. He had come to believe that "art could not be separated from the overall phenomenon of life."[3] The question was how to integrate the two?

In 1967 Pesce and Vettore visited Cesare Cassina with some design ideas. Cassina took the two on a tour of the factory. During the visit, a high-pitched noise emitted by one of the machines caused Vettore to suffer a brain hemorrhage, killing her. It shook Pesce deeply. "I'm sure," he says, "over the next years, all the work I did where blood was very present had to do with this."

The first of these truly gory creations was *Pièce per una Fucilazione* (Piece for an Execution by Shooting), a theater work performed in Padua in 1967 and later in Helsinki. In it, a man is executed by gunshot and the audience watches as he "bleeds" to death; he bleeds so long and so copiously that the blood flows off the stage onto the floor and into the seated audience. "Theater cannot include only people," says Pesce. "What acts on stage is matter."[4]

If the period after graduation had felt like one of fallow, it proved to be one of gestation. Many of Pesce's ideas were now coalescing into challenging original forms, coinciding with the late sixties, an era of questioning and rebellion. All of this turbulent energy was animating Italian design. Many young politicized Italian designers felt torn between their fascination for the boundless products being manufactured by a fledgling consumer society and the banality and superficiality they represented. Attempting to find some deeper purpose to their role than mere problem solvers, they sought to imbue the objects they created with meaning and emotion. This "counterdesign movement" would be known as Radical Architecture. Pesce would succeed in being not only a leader of the counterdesign movement, but also its antagonist. Although he was struggling with the same social, cultural, and political issues as his peers, he saw his quest to literally re-form design as a solitary one.

While some Italian designers were creating works that possessed true individuality, in an attempt to establish what designer Andrea Branzi called a "renewed rationalism,"[5] Pesce was proposing that objects *were* individuals. Like people, they too were "asking to be different, to be free." **Sameness for Pesce meant "bondage." He wanted to mass manufacture originals, to produce a diversified series of objects, and so reconnect craft with industry. This, he believed, would constitute "a deep revolution in industry . . . a third industrial revolution."** Achieving this capacity would enable society to break out of the constrictions of mass production and so address the needs of a more individualized marketplace. He saw this changing market in the way the "flower children" were customizing their cars and other industrial products. Many of these convictions would be expressed in his first collection of furnishings, the technically astonishing Up series.

Like Archimedes, Pesce had his eureka moment while bathing. He was suddenly struck by the expansive qualities of his sponge. Soon after, he proposed to Cassina the idea for a line of furnishings made entirely out of high-density molded polyurethane foam, without any internal structure. This was already a technologically daring notion, but

Pesce went further. He suggested that after the foam chairs were upholstered in a stretch fabric, they be flattened by sucking the air out of them in a vacuum, then heat-sealed flat between vinyl sheets. When removed from this vinyl packaging, the foam furnishings would slowly inflate back to their original shape. Storage and shipping would be simple and economical.

In addition to simple chair and love seat forms, Pesce wanted to fabricate an "anti-armchair" in the figure of a reclining ancient fertility goddess, its ample bosoms the headrest, its deep lap the seat. Attached to La Mamma, as he called it, was a chain connecting the chair to an upholstered foam ball ottoman. (The chain was later replaced with a long cord by the manufacturer; today the pieces are sold separately.) He also wanted to produce a giant-sized foot just because he could.

Cassina, a man of both progressive outlook and pragmatism, agreed to the project, including the latter two pieces as long as they weren't any more expensive to manufacture. They weren't, but producing La Mamma's complex form proved a technical challenge. Pesce consulted with Bayer, the foam manufacturer, on how to go about the process, as it would require injecting forty kilos of polyurethane into the mold in one shot. "Impossible" was the answer. Pesce was undeterred. "I started to study [the material and process] in the factory and I found a way to use the polyurethane that people had never done before," he recalls. "It's a good attitude to doubt rules. Creativity doesn't follow rules." For Pesce, discovering what to do with new materials like polyurethane foam is one of the designer's most critical social roles. The Up series debuted at the 1969 Salone del Mobile in Milan.

With La Mamma, Pesce transformed a design object into a politically and socially charged work of sculpture, which, striking for its time, was unabashedly figural. He called it "a document of reality." The disparateness of the Up series was equally polemical. **Like many of his radical colleagues, Pesce was calling for furnishings**

"no longer with precise laws (may all legislators be damned!) that impose obsolete and often segregating and categorical ways of life, but a free set of things from which, whether they are period or contemporary, one can demand an everyday psychological presence."[6]

Pesce presented the Up series with an ornately illustrated manifesto, depicting the furnishings emerging out of some cosmic goo. He also created the advertising for the series, having the different pieces of Up shot inside a sensuously formed cavern. The publicity photographs featured the furniture surrounded by models clad in exotic catsuits in fantastical vignettes best described as Fellini meets Barbarella. They were shot like fashion photography because Pesce considers fashion a powerful medium for communication. It is, for him, a form of art.

Other works of psychological presence and provocation quickly followed. "Research really makes sense," says Pesce, "only if it is resolutely innovative, and innovation really makes sense only if it's resolutely disturbing."[7] Invited in 1969 by the Italian manufacturer Gabbianelli to propose new ideas for ashtrays, Pesce sent off the prototype Manodidio (Hand of God), a bloody palm with a stigmata as the ash receptacle. It was not produced. "It was a provocation to the company, and to people who were believers," says Pesce with a smile of satisfaction. "It was provoking and functional; that is hard to do." That year as the Christmas gift for Cassina's clients, he created Fioreinbocca (Flower in Mouth), a polyurethane bas-relief of a face with a flower in the mouth and blood streaming from the nose. Cesare Cassina was understandably nervous about it. But he was urged on by Mario Bellini and Vico Magistretti, two of the titans of Italian Rationalism. Their early support still gratifies Pesce.

Many of Pesce's early designs refer to the perfectly proportioned human form of the Renaissance, once employed as a measure for all things. But such perfection troubled him. "Human beings are full of mistakes," he says. "For me

it was important to use the mistake as a quality. To find a different kind of beauty." Other cultures, especially primitive cultures, depicted less ideal human forms in their art. Why not, when creating a new domestic landscape, use this kind of form as the measure? La Mamma was Pesce's first attempt to do this. Another was Yeti. Manufactured in a limited edition by Cassina in 1969, Yeti was an upholstered foam armchair, possibly for a deformed giant as it was huge in scale and asymmetrical, with arms of different heights and widths.

Pesce followed it in 1970 with Moloch, an enormous desk lamp, whose towering size liberates it from its "tasks." It was produced by Bracciodiffero, a company Pesce helped found with Cesare Cassina and Cassina's art director, Francesco Binfaré. Bracciodiffero was the first experimental furniture company of its kind. Dedicated to promoting cutting-edge design and its audience, in its brief but incandescent life, it produced some of the most avant-garde objects of its era, works by Pesce, Alessandro Mendini, and the Cuban designer Riccardo Porro. (After its closing, Mendini would in 1976 help found another experimental furniture company, Studio Alchimia, which later spawned Memphis.)

That year the progressive Musée des Arts Decoratifs in Paris offered the thirty-one-year-old Pesce a one-man exhibition, for which he devised a series of art installations made atmospheric by the piped-in chanting of Buddhist monks intermixed with meditative electronic music of his own composing, and the scent of sandalwood incense. To see the La Mamma chair, visitors entered an improvised prison cell, complete with the sound of a creaking metal door. The show was widely covered by the press. La Mamma and Yeti riled the Leftist papers, which were offended by Pesce's affirmation of diversity.

In 1972 Bracciodiffero produced another Pesce masterwork, the Golgotha suite. Harkening back again to the Renaissance, this time to its biblically themed art and objects, Pesce took the Passion of Christ as his subject for a banquet-sized table and dining chairs. The table was constructed upside down out of dark rubber bricks

mortared together with a blood-red gel coat that, when turned right-side up, "bled" up onto the tabletop. The chairs were made of a fiberglass cloth that was bathed in polyester resin, hung on wire hooks, and draped into the form of a chair. The rigidity of each chair depended upon the duration of the fabric's soaking. Some chairs were strong enough to support a person; other "deformed" versions retained their shape but crumpled to the ground. These were the first of Pesce's designs to fully realize his notion of an industrially produced "series of originals."

Following on the heels of the show came an invitation from Emilio Ambasz, a curator of architecture and design at New York's Museum of Modern Art, to participate in "The New Domestic Landscape," what would be a landmark exhibition on contemporary Italian design. As a special feature, Ambasz wanted Pesce along with many of the elite of the design communities of Florence and Milan to create environments representative of their visions.

Pesce presented an installation in the daring form of a fictional archaeological reconstruction. The scenario involved archaeologists sometime in the third millennium discovering in the southern European Alps a small subterranean city from the late second millennium, the period known as the "Age of the Great Contamination." The people had moved into deep pits sealing themselves off from the outside world. The environment they created was a sterile, claustrophobic assemblage of rigid geometries. Also exhibited was a "discovered" videotape, entitled "Paesaggio Domestico"

(Domestic Landscape), in which members from a subterranean "commune" feast on one of their own in a ritualized ceremony. From these alarming discoveries, the archaeologists speculated that this had been a neurotic, highly rationalist civilization that had turned backward upon itself.

There were other highly conceptual, socially provocative environments in the show, but none were as openly adversarial or graphic as Pesce's installation. Ambasz diplomatically situated it away from the others; he even set it apart in the show's catalogue, under the heading "Design as Commentary." After the exhibition closed, the museum informed Pesce that owing to some customs restrictions, it would not be able to return the installation to him, but would have to destroy it. A reprieve came at the last minute, when the Musée des Arts Decoratifs purchased the work.

In the early 1970s, when not creating controversy, Pesce advanced his research into the making of industrial originals. Still based in Paris, he was traveling regularly and spending the summers in Venice, where he worked on projects at his workshop with his wife, Francesca Lucco, and a changing band of students and admirers. The furniture that came out of this fertile period further demonstrated Pesce's wondrous, deviant resourcefulness and his interest in the latest artistic currents. Playing with a favorite material of Arte Povera, Pesce took rags soaked in polyurethane, and crafted them into substantial armchairs and bookcases. Continuing to experiment with polyurethane, he cast a bookcase from a mold without airholes. Called the Carenza, it resembles a demolished wall, the rough edges of its shelves and posts the result of fissures in the material made by the trapped air. Normally such defects would put a manufacturer to shame; here they are what gives the piece character.

As much as Pesce experimented with these contemporary technologies, he couldn't, and wouldn't, remove the artisan's hand from them. The carnality and sensuality of the materials was essential to him. By creating objects infused with human touch and, later, choice, Pesce was feminizing industry, softening the numbing "male" precision of its mechanisms. In the following years Pesce would devise techniques by which unskilled laborers could become artisans. He saw these flawed objects as "documents of reality," and therefore beautiful. Noteworthy in this research were his Sansone tables I, II (1980, 1987), the Pratt chair series (1984), and his glass experiments at CIRVA (1988–1991; CIRVA is the French acronym for Marseilles's International Center for Glass and Plastic Arts). The latter he called these projects his investigations into the "mal fait" (badly made).

He had not yet devised the term, but the precedent piece for the *mal fait* was the Sit Down suite. An upholstered polyurethane armchair and love seat, manufactured by Cassina in 1975, it marked another technological breakthrough. Dispensing with conventional molds, Pesce used only a simple wood frame and strong canvas upholstery to shape the injected polyurethane. Though sturdy and functional, the pieces were imperfect, possessing similar but not identical shapes, owing to the fabric's random folds during the injection molding. Through this technique foam furniture could be manufactured inexpensively, but Cassina presented them as high-priced "avant-garde" furnishings.

Pesce's captivation with the unbeautiful has never diminished his ability to make gorgeous objects. His molded polyurethane Wan-Chai chair (1986–1987) is lovely, lyrical, and a technical tour de force. While the chair's base is rigid enough to support a sitter, its seat and back are pliable for comfortable sitting. Sweetly arranged on the seat are a few pieces of fruit, which transform the simple chair into a sculptural still life. Inspiration for the work came from Rauschenberg's three-dimensional canvases. "I thought why not make a three-dimensional volume that looks like a chair, a canvas that is carrying a still life," Pesce recalls. "I wanted to continue the idea of the object as an expression of art."

Pesce believes there is a danger to our love of beauty. It is a prison from which he wants to liberate us. What better tools than shock and repulsion for breaking us out of restrictive behaviors and antiquated values? "We work for people," he declares. "In our time, creators have forgotten that our work is done for others."[8]

In 1975 Pesce had another show at the Musée des Arts Decoratifs. Entitled "Le Futur est Peut-être Passé?" (The Future Is Perhaps Passed?), it would be the most controversial yet. Again, Pesce challenged the supremacy of rationalist thinking, especially its oppressive definition of time and humanity. Among the pieces on display was a Tinguely-like contraption entitled *Machine to Measure a Lifetime*. This "clock" marks time within an eighty-year span—an approximate human life—instead of in repetitive hourly intervals. "Time is never the same," says Pesce. He marked time more viscerally in another piece, his *Appearances of Time (Homage to Mies van der Rohe)* made literally from viscera. For the opening, Pesce used fresh meat to make models of the architectural works of Mies van der Rohe; these were then displayed in glass vitrines. "I wanted to show that people can decompose when they live in a certain kind of space," he explains.

While the displays looked completely sealed, as the museum had requested, Pesce had in fact put small holes in the bottom. The first visitors may have been stunned by the display, but those who came in the ensuing days were increasingly repelled, not only by what Pesce remembers as the "fantastic" colors of the decomposing meat, but by the putrid odor from the liquids dripping discreetly out of the cases onto the carpeting below. The smell soon pervaded not only the exhibition gallery, but other rooms within the museum and its offices. It became so bad that two weeks after the exhibition opened, the museum guards and employees, unable to endure it any longer, went on strike. The exhibition was closed amid a media uproar. The sensation, says Pesce, on strike. The exhibition was closed amid a media uproar. The sensation, says Pesce, "helped me to understand that creativity could continue to 'disturb,' if it moved along the road of a strong, material sacredness."[9]

Pesce was growing famous in Europe but not rich. "I was always out of money," he says. "I was focused on research, not on coming out with a new model every year." He now had two small children, and his need for some regular income had grown acute. Help came in the unlikely form of the French Ministry of Culture. Rather than shrinking from Pesce and his attack against the very foundations of French intellectual culture—Cartesian Rationalism—it embraced him. The ministry offered Pesce an apartment in Paris and a tenured professorship at an architecture school in either Paris or Strasbourg. As he had never visited Strasbourg, Pesce chose its Institut d'Architecture et d'Etudes Urbaines.

In 1979 Pesce was one of several architects invited to participate in the exhibition "Transformations in Modern Architecture" at New York's MoMA. According to the letter of invitation, it was intended to be an exploration of non-reductionist architecture. Pesce proposed replacing the Seagram Building, one of Mies van der Rohe's masterpieces, with a high-rise of cast polyurethane pieces in the shape of organic architectural forms and body parts, piled one on top of the other, and then hollowed out to form interior living spaces. As illustration, he presented a rubber model about ten feet tall. It was especially incendiary because Philip Johnson, the original director of the museum's architecture department, had not only coined the term "International Style" in a landmark architectural show there, but had also collaborated with Mies on the design of the Seagram Building. Pesce's submission was rejected, but he refused to accept defeat. He rallied the press and appealed, with the subtle support of one of his collectors who was a museum trustee, to the MoMA's director, Richard Oldenberg. Ultimately, his model was displayed, but like his previous MoMA experience, it was

Pesce would continue to develop the notion of a nonhomogeneous or "disobedient" architecture in his counterproposal for Les Halles in 1979 and for a residential tower in São Paolo in 1987. Both involved constructing residential buildings whose structures would be empty concrete platforms, equipped only with basic technical systems. Apartment buyers would purchase a section and then hire an architect to design and construct a home on it. His inspiration came from the high-rises he had seen in Hong Kong, where residents in need of more space had built out enclosed terraces in a variety of styles and materials, unintentionally providing formerly anonymous buildings with highly eccentric facades.

In 1980 Pesce accepted an invitation to lecture at New York's Pratt Institute and moved his family from Paris to New York. The city has since become the nexus of his operations. During this period, he pursued his research into the diversified series with the Sansone II tables and the Pratt series of chairs. "Unskilled" laborers made the objects and determined aspects of their appearance.

He would take the "diversified series" in another direction with his Unequal suite, presented by Cassina at the 1987 Salone del Mobile. The pieces of this suite, a wardrobe, a table, a modular sofa, and an armchair, share little in regard to style or form. And the seating modules that make up the sofa, called Cannaregio, are dissimiliar. They can be conjoined, though they don't fit neatly together—much like the individualistic palazzi in that Venetian quarter—or they can be arranged separately like people at a cocktail party. The Il Feltro armchair, by contrast, made of felt as its name suggests, looks like a highly refined version of a shaman's throne. The thick wool felt of the chair's base is soaked in polyester resin in the same process used for the Golgotha chair, and then shaped on a mold. Coated with resin, the fabric base becomes strong enough to hold its shape and the weight of a person, while the top fabric remains malleable. The chair enfolds the sitter like a coat—Pesce again plays with fashion—and conforms to his shape, changing each time it is sat upon. The theme of envelopment recurs throughout Pesce's oeuvre. Sometimes the theme is comforting, as with La Mamma and Il Feltro, other times disturbingly claustrophobic as in the *City for an Age of Contaminations*, where the dwellers were partially swallowed into the walls.

As with so many of his designs, Pesce hoped that by using low-tech, inexpensive processes, Il Feltro could be mass produced in some underdeveloped country, perhaps out of cast-off rugs, and then widely distributed. Cassina again was not interested in such an arrangement. "I remember them telling me that they were obligated to take care of their own workers," says Pesce. Today, the chairs are exquisitely crafted out of thick felt and priced accordingly.

During the eighties, Pesce also conducted research into lighting fixtures. These functional sculptures resemble extraterrestrials with wood-knobbed antennae and brick-shaped feet and have bodies made of flexible polyurethane resin set in an electrified wire grid. Their cartoonish appearance marked a departure for Pesce, whose work, while often congenial, had never been overtly friendly. Beginning with the Dalila chairs from 1980, Pesce's furnishings began to sport not just faces, but smiling ones. A smile is a universal symbol and this interests Pesce immensely. "The image, not writing, is the most important carrier of a culture," he explains, which in turn explains his interest in fashion photography. "It is also more democratic than writing." And what form of image is more widely understood than the cartoon?

Despite the new direction his work was taking, Pesce hadn't lost his appetite for provocation in the face of an obdurately abstract world. **At the end of the 1980s he created the Knife lamp, a giant-sized knife that stabs the wall, with light streaming from its "wound." Referring to the work in a 1991 interview, he said: "Both architecture and design, as they are still thought of today, are**

extremely abstract. Personally I seek a violent relationship with them, which is a knife planted into a wall."[10]

As with so much of Pesce's work, the light fixtures evolved out of the development of yet another production technique. Called Open Sky, it is a half-mold process for polyurethane castings that Pesce began experimenting with on the roof above his SoHo studio, hence the name. It enabled him to create plastic forms that were soft in texture, remarkably flexible, and extraordinarily translucent and colorful. Yet another process that didn't require a skilled artisan, the Open Sky products could be easily manufactured, so Pesce produced them out of his own studio. This collection and another previously developed one, called Fish Design, made of hand-cast translucent and opaque resins, and ranging from chairs to jewelry, he priced affordably and geared toward youthful buyers.

Keeping to his credo of incoherence, in 1994 Pesce came up with a nifty work of engineering. He had become interested in the conventions of the folding seat. Why did it *have* to look like a chair? Why should it be hidden away in the closet? As an alternative, Pesce designed a folding stool for the Italian furniture manufacturer Zerodisegno in the shape of a cute mini umbrella, transforming the chair type into a fashion accessory. In keeping with Pesce's manufacturing philosophy, Zerodisegno let the factory workers choose the color combinations of the stool's plastic handle and seat. Pesce worked again with Zerodisegno on Nobody's Perfect, which was introduced at the 2002 Salone del Mobile. The collection consists of twelve separately shaped panels, each made from a large drop of plastic resin. The pieces can be variously combined to create shelves, chairs, tables, etc. Customers can buy the panels according to their different needs. What better way to address an ever-fragmenting marketplace?

Some of Pesce's most interesting work from the nineties involved the design of environments, including a retrospective show at the Centre Georges Pompidou in 1996.

Called "Les Temps des Questions," (The Time of Questions), its layout was in the combined image of a woman's profile and a question mark. The creator of this show was a more mellow Pesce than the one who had last had a museum show in Paris; there were no works of outrageous provocation. Instead, the reassuring aroma of minestrone wafted through the exhibition rooms. However, those rooms were made out of sandbags, so the exhibition space resembled a makeshift fortress. Visitors had to make their way through the barricades and then scout out all the works in the labyrinthine layout. Pesce expects a lot from museum-goers: He hoped they would come back several times to the exhibition to see different parts when in different moods.

Environmentalists were in no mood to accept his project for Avignon's Expo of Beauty in 2000. It consisted of several small buildings crafted from unlikely building materials: a souvenir stand made out of silicone, a snack stand from extruded silicone, a guard house from rigid foam, and rest rooms from poured polyurethane. All these materials are environmentally noxious. By proposing them as the building materials of the future, Pesce inflamed the Green Party; its protests quashed the project. Pesce openly acknowledges plastic's problematic nature in regard to the environment, and the reality of looming global environmental crises. He nevertheless insists on the correctness of his continued research into plastics. "Materials are capable of incredible development. Compared to wood or stone, plastic is a young material," he says. "When electricity was discovered, it was potentially dangerous. . . . Progress is one of the main reasons why we are here." Michael Sorkin, an architecture critic and a friend of Pesce's, suggests that he "requires a material that may not yet exist."

Meanwhile, Pesce has gone about his research in a land where environmentalists have little political say. Like an architectural Fitzcarraldo, he has journeyed to Brazil to realize his vision. In Salvadore, a seaside town in Bahia, he is slowly building a vacation compound for himself and friends made out of a variety of eclectic building materials. The compound consists of a main house and seven satellite guest houses, each composed out of a different material, and all perched on stilts and connected to one another by wooden walkways. The building materials include natural rubber, recycled industrial rubber, rigid polyurethane foam, shot polyurethane, poured polyurethane, silicone bricks, injected silicone, and cement mixed with earth and grain, so that the walls will grow plants. When finished an aerial view of the arrangement of buildings will reveal a profile of Pesce, the creator.

This is a brave work of experimentation, especially for the houseguests. Pesce relates that when he began to build the natural rubber house—its walls to be as soft as skin—he realized it would also smell like rubber. He consulted a local rubber plantation, and learned that the workers wash their hands in juniper juice to stanch the odor. He went back and added juniper juice to his rubber mixture. "Now we have a house that opens up your sinuses!" he exclaims. "We made this kind of discovery to help people live better—the possibilities of new materials to be discovered are limitless."[11] In the far reaches of Brazil, Gaetano Pesce goes on charting new territories.

● Bahia House drawing,
1995–97

The first of these truly gory creations was *Pièce per una Fucilazione* (Piece for an Execution by Shooting), a theater work performed in Padua in 1967. In it, a man is executed by gunshot and the audience watches as he "bleeds" to death; he bleeds so long and so copiously that the blood flows off the stage onto the floor and into the seated audience. "Theater cannot include only people," says Pesce. "What acts on stage is matter."

Piece for an Execution
by Shooting,
1967

Manodidio (Hand of
God) for Gabbianelli,
1969

Fioreinbocca (Flower
in Mouth) for Cassina,
1969

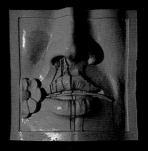

- Up series and Yeti poster, 1969

- Yeti armchair for Cassina, 1968

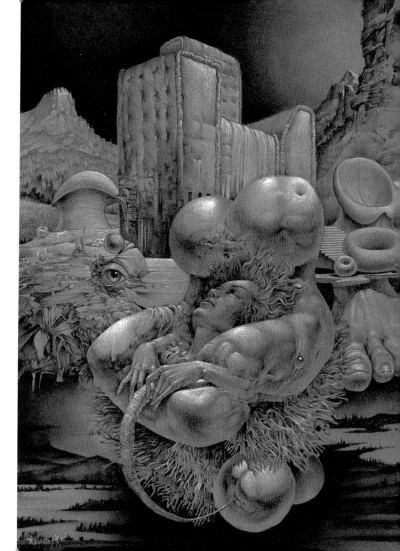

● *Reconstruction
of an Underground
City—Fragments,
1971–72*

| 33 |

● Door project,
   1972

● Project for the
   Chicago Tribune,
   1980

The publicity photographs featured the furniture surrounded by models clad in exotic catsuits in fantastical vignettes best described as Fellini meets Barbarella. They were shot like fashion photography because Pesce considers fashion a powerful medium for communication.

- LEFT:
  Up series No. 5 and
  No. 6 La Mamma,
  1969

- ABOVE:
  Up series No. 7
  Il Pied, 1969

- FOLLOWING PAGES:
  Publicity photo for
  Up series, 1969

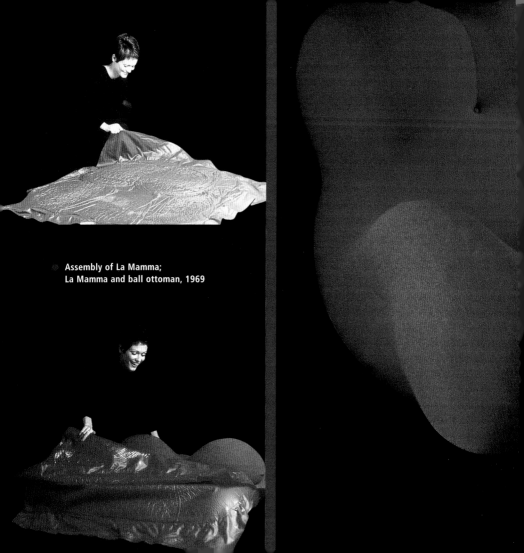

Assembly of La Mamma;
La Mamma and ball ottoman, 1969

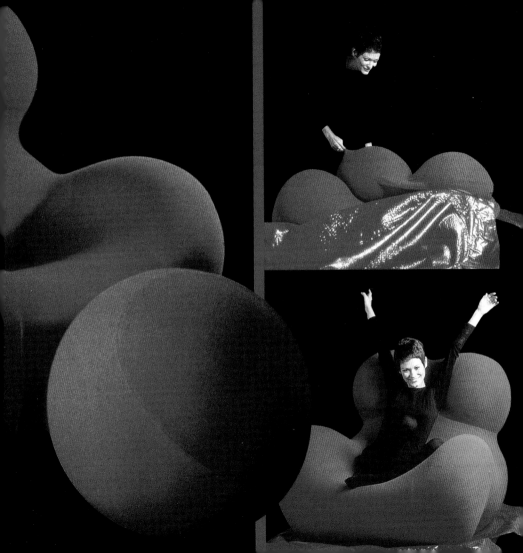

Il Pugno (the Fist)
love seat, 1971–72

● Sit Down armchair;
  Assembly process for
  Cassina, 1975–80

Dispensing with conventional molds, Pesce used only a simple wood frame and strong canvas upholstery to shape the injected polyurethane. Though sturdy and functional, the pieces were imperfect, possessing similar but not identical shapes, owing to the fabric's random folds during the injection molding.

● FOLLOWING PAGES: (LEFT)
  Rag armchair, 1972

● FOLLOWING PAGES: (RIGHT)
  La Differenza è Vita
  installation for the
  Verenezia exhibition,
  Palazzo Grassi, Venice,
  1980

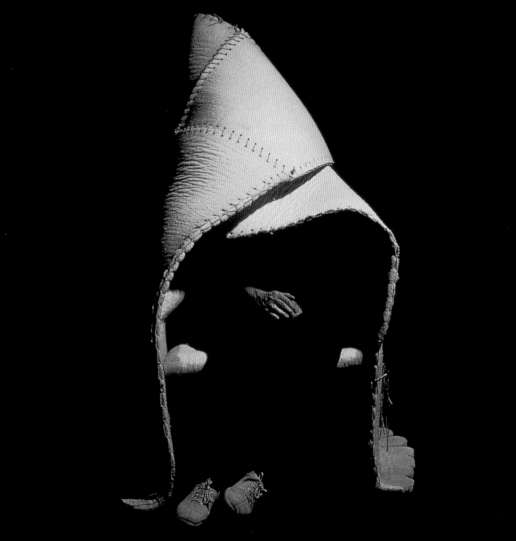

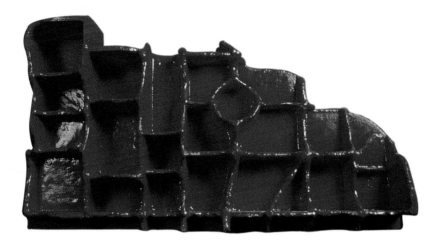

Pesce cast a bookcase from a mold without air-holes. Called the Carenza, it resembles a demolished wall, the rough edges of its shelves and posts the result of fissures in the material made by the trapped air. Normally such defects would put a manufacturer to shame; here they are what gives the piece character.

● PREVIOUS PAGES:
I Feltri felt armchairs
for Cassina, 1986–87

● LEFT AND ABOVE:
Carenza bookshelf,
1972 and 1975

● FOLLOWING PAGES:
The Golgotha suite
for Bracciodiffero,
1972–73

Dalila chair, 1980

Garden armchair
in rubber, 1984

| 54 |

FOLLOWING PAGES:
Pratt chair series,
1984

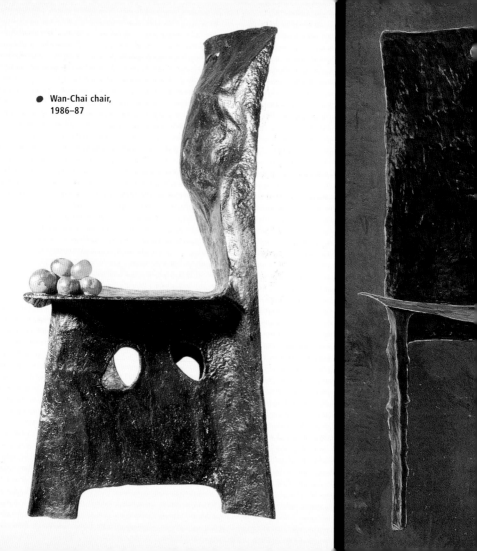

Wan-Chai chair,
1986–87

- Pesce working with resin material

- TOP LEFT TO RIGHT:
  Vesuvio coffeepot prototype for Zani & Zani SpA, 1992

  Resin skin portrait, 1980

  Rag lamp No. 3 for Fish Design, 1995–99

  Feat vase, 1999

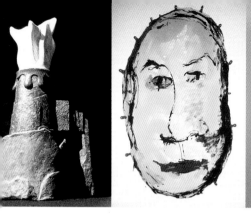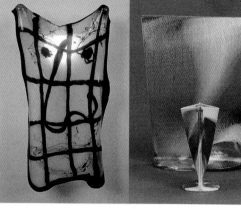

Pesce was proposing that objects *were* individuals. Like people, they too were "asking to be different, to be free." Sameness for Pesce meant "bondage." He wanted to mass manufacture originals, to produce a diversified series of objects, and so reconnect craft with industry.

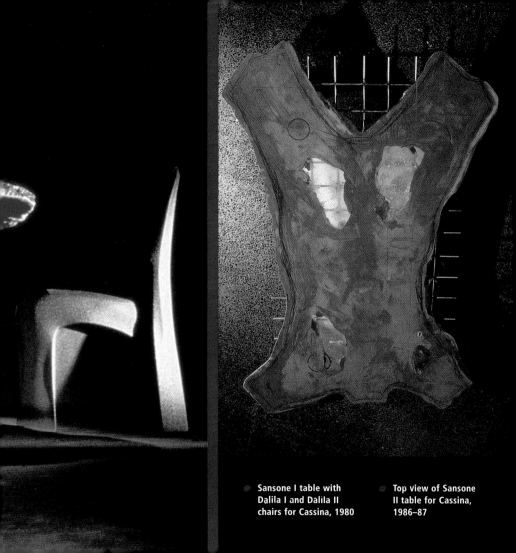

Sansone I table with Dalila I and Dalila II chairs for Cassina, 1980

Top view of Sansone II table for Cassina, 1986–87

● Table with 12 legs,
1991

● Green Street chair,
1984

● FOLLOWING PAGES: (LEFT)
Umbrella chair for
Zerodisegno, 1992

● FOLLOWING PAGES: (RIGHT)
543 Broadway chairs
for Bernini, 1992

● Pair of Baby Crosby
  chairs, 1999.
  Production Open Sky.

● FAR RIGHT:
  Nobody's Perfect
  collection for
  Zerodisegno, 2002

Pesce working in
the CIRVA Glass
Factory

TOP RIGHT:
Bautta mask and
No. 158 for CIRVA
Glass Factory,
1988–1992

As much as Pesce experimented with these contemporary technologies, he couldn't, and wouldn't, remove the artisan's hand from them. The carnality and sensuality of the materials was essential to him. By creating objects infused with human touch, and later choice, Pesce was feminizing industry, softening the numbing "male" precision of its mechanisms.

● Mineral water bottle for Vittel, 1986–89

● FAR RIGHT:
Petit Pave Blue
for CIRVA Glass
Factory, 1988–92

● Caffè Florian goblet
for the Venice Biennale,
1994–95

● Knife lamp,
  1989–91

Referring to the work in a 1991 interview, Pesce said: "Both architecture and design, as they are still thought of today, are extremely abstract.

Personally I seek a violent relationship with them, which is a knife planted into a wall."

● Heart Lamp,
1979–80

● Genesi? (Hiroshima)
lamp, 1973

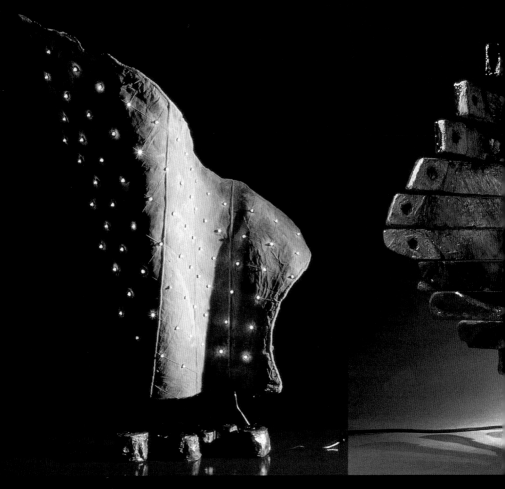

Airport lamp,
1986

Portrait lamp,
1989

Tree lamp,
1992

Bastone lamp,
1986

Rag lamp for
Fish Design,
1995–99

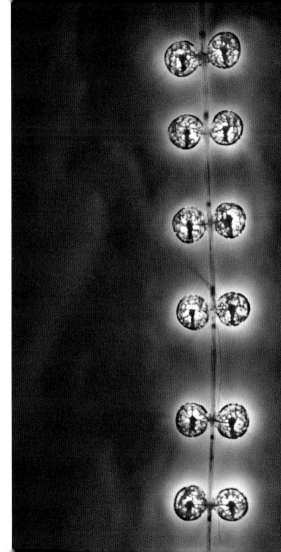

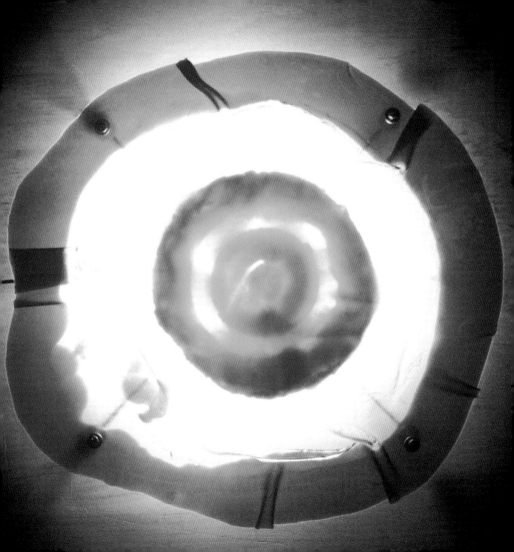

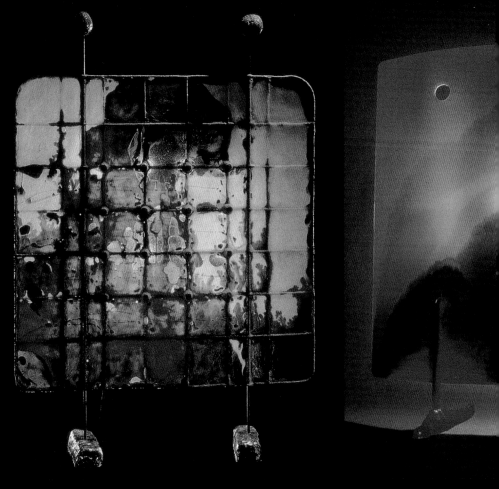

Square lamp,
1986

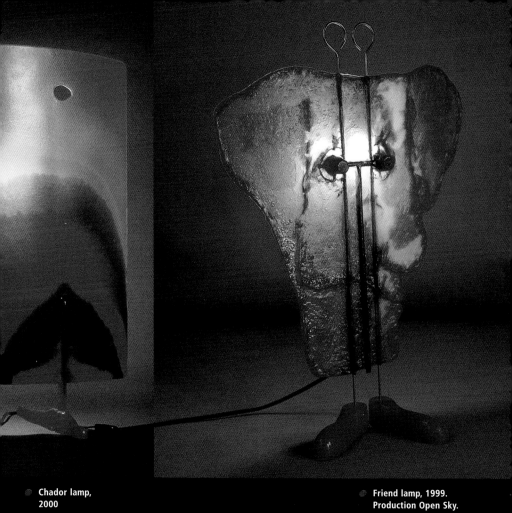

Chador lamp,
2000

Friend lamp, 1999.
Production Open Sky.

Jay Chiat of the hip ad agency Chiat/Day wanted
to create the first "virtual workplace" designed
around technology. He wanted a headquarters
that would do away with paper and architectural hierarchies and encourage more creative
interactions. What better architect for the project than Pesce?

● Chiat/Day office in
   New York, 1994

● FOLLOWING PAGES:
   Chiat/Day cafeteria,
   1994

Moscow hotel room for the
Grand Hotel Salone at Milan's
Salone del Mobile, 2002

Some of Pesce's most interesting work from the nineties involved the design of environments, including a retrospective show at the Centre Georges Pompidou in 1996. Called "Les Temps des Questions," (The Time of Questions), its layout was in the combined image of a woman's profile and a question mark.

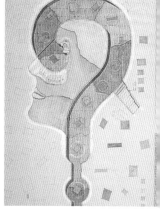

● "Gaetano Pesce, Le Temps des Questions" exhibit and plan at the Centre Georges Pompidou in Paris, 1996

● Arbitare Italia System
  Casa, 1991

GAETANO PESCE BIOGRAPHY

1939   Born on November 2 in La Spezia

1957   First solo gallery show at Pro Padova Gallery, Padua

1959   Enters the Faculty of Architecture at the University of Venice. Cofounds Gruppo N.

1961   Quits Gruppo N

1964   Meets Cesare Cassina of the contemporary furniture manufacturing firm, Cassina SpA

1965   Graduates from Faculty of Architecture, at the University of Venice

1967   Stages his multimedia theater work, *Pièce per una Fucilazione,* in Padua. Creates Yeti armchair, prototype, for Cassina, Meda/Milan

1969   Creates Up series for C&B Italia, Novedrate/Como. Lectures about Italian design in Tokyo and Kyoto

1970   Cofounds Bracciodiffero, an experimental furniture company, with Cesare Cassina and Francesco Binfaré. "Nouveau Espaces," one-man show at Musée des Art Decoratifs, Paris. Creates Moloch lamp, small series, for Bracciodiffero, Genoa. Stages *Piéce per una Fucilazione* in Helsinki

1971   Lectures at the International Design Conference, Aspen, Colorado

1972   Participates in "Italy: The New Domestic Landscape" at the Museum of Modern Art, New York City. Creates Golgotha suite for Bracciodiffero, Genoa. Creates Carenza book-case, prototype

1975   Creates Sit Down suite for Cassina, Meda/Milan. "Le Futur est peut-être Passé?" one-man show at Musée des Art Decoratifs, Paris. Becomes professor at Institut d'Architecture et d'Etudes Urbaines, Strasbourg, France

1979   Invited to participate in "Transformations in Modern Architecture" at the Museum of Modern Art, New York City. Participates in competition for the development of Les Halles, Paris

1980   Lectures at the Architecture School, Pratt Institute, New York City. Creates Dalila chairs

1982   Creates Pratt chair series

1986   Creates Wan-Chai chair (Homage to Hong Kong), small series. Designs Mineral water bottle for Vittel

1987   Creates Unequal suite: I Feltri armchairs, Cannaregio modular sofa, Sansone II tables, and Les Ateliers armoire for Cassina, Meda/Milan

1988   Designs Non-Homogeneous Tower prototype, São Paolo, Brazil

1989   Creates Portrait lamp, prototype

1990   Researches new glass techniques with CIRVA, Marseille, France

1991   Develops Open Sky technique

1992   Designs Umbrella chair for Zerodisegno, Alessandria, Italy

1994   Designs Chiat/Day offices, New York City. Creates Caffè Florian goblet for the Venice Biennale. Establishes Fish Design series of products

1995   Embarks on design and construction of vacation compound, Salvatore, Bahia, Brazil

1996   "Les Temps des Questions," retrospective show at at the Centre Georges Pompidou

2002   Designs Nobody's Perfect collection for Zerodisegno, Alessandria, Italy. Designs Moscow hotel room for Grand Hotel Salone, Salone del Mobile, Milan

NOTES

1. Gaetano Pesce, *An Architectural Project for a Highrise in Manhattan,* poster manifesto (New York: Museum of Modern Art, 1979).

2. *Gaetano Pesce: Multidisciplinary Work,* exhibition catalogue (Tel Aviv: Tel Aviv Museum of Art, Peter Joseph Gallery,1991), p. 15.

3. Ibid, p. 15.

4. Ibid, p. 17.

5. Jocelyn de Noblet, ed., *Industrial Design: Reflections of a Century,* (Paris: Flammarion/APCI, 1993), p. 259.

6. "Perpetual Creativity," *Interior View #15,* January 2000, p. 59.

7. *Gaetano Pesce: Multidisciplinary Work,* p. 17.

8. Ibid, p. 38.

9. Ibid, p. 17.

10. Ibid, p. 23.

11. "Perpetual Creativity," p. 60.

INDEX